Irvine

by Iain Gray

Lang**Syne**

PUBLISHING

WRITING *to* REMEMBER

LangSyne

PUBLISHING

WRITING *to* REMEMBER

Vineyard Business Centre,
Pathhead, Midlothian EH37 5XP
Tel: 01875 321 203 Fax: 01875 321 233
E-mail: info@lang-syne.co.uk
www.langsyneshop.co.uk

Design by Dorothy Meikle
Printed by Ricoh Print Scotland
© Lang Syne Publishers Ltd 2011

ISBN 978-1-85217-228-2

Irvine

MOTTO:
Flourishing in both sunshine and in shade.

CREST:
A sheaf of holly.

TERRITORY:
Dumfriesshire and Aberdeenshire.

Echoes of a far distant past
can still be found in most names

Chapter one:

Origins of Scottish surnames

by George Forbes

It all began with the Normans.

For it was they who introduced surnames into common usage more than a thousand years ago, initially based on the title of their estates, local villages and chateaux in France to distinguish and identify these landholdings, usually acquired at the point of a bloodstained sword.

Such grand descriptions also helped enhance the prestige of these arrogant warlords and generally glorify their lofty positions high above the humble serfs slaving away below in the pecking order who only had single names, often with Biblical connotations as in Pierre and Jacques.

The only descriptive distinctions

among this peasantry concerned their occupations, like Pierre the swineherd or Jacques the ferryman.

The Normans themselves were originally Vikings (or Northmen) who raided, colonised and eventually settled down around the French coastline.

They had sailed up the Seine in their longboats in 900AD under their ferocious leader Rollo and ruled the roost in north east France before sailing over to conquer England, bringing their relatively new tradition of having surnames with them.

It took another hundred years for the Normans to percolate northwards and surnames did not begin to appear in Scotland until the thirteenth century.

These adventurous knights brought an aura of chivalry with them and it was said no damsel of any distinction would marry a man unless he had at least two names.

The family names included that of Scotland's great hero Robert De Brus and his compatriots were warriors from families like the De Morevils, De Umphravils, De Berkelais, De Quincis, De Viponts and De Vaux.

As the knights settled the boundaries of their vast estates, they took territorial names, as in Hamilton, Moray, Crawford, Cunningham, Dunbar, Ross, Wemyss, Dundas, Galloway, Renfrew, Greenhill, Hazelwood, Sandylands and Church-hill.

Other names, though not with any obvious geographical or topographical features, nevertheless derived from ancient parishes like Douglas, Forbes, Dalyell and Guthrie.

Other surnames were coined in connection with occupations, castles or legendary deeds. Stuart originated in the word steward, a prestigious post which was an integral part of any large medieval household. The same applied to Cooks, Chamberlains, Constables and Porters.

Borders towns and forts - needed in

areas like the Debateable Lands which were constantly fought over by feuding local families - had their own distinctive names; and it was often from them that the resident groups took their communal titles, as in the Grahams of Annandale, the Elliots and Armstrongs of the East Marches, the Scotts and Kerrs of Teviotdale and Eskdale.

Even physical attributes crept into surnames, as in Small, Little and More (the latter being 'beg' in Gaelic), Long or Lang, Stark, Stout, Strong or Strang and even Jolly.

Mieklejohns would have had the strength of several men, while Littlejohn was named after the legendary sidekick of Robin Hood.

Colours got into the act with Black, White, Grey, Brown and Green (Red developed into Reid, Ruddy or Ruddiman). Blue was rare and nobody ever wanted to be associated with yellow.

Pompous worthies took the name Wiseman, Goodman and Goodall.

Words intimating the sons of leading figures were soon affiliated into the language as in Johnson, Adamson, Richardson and Thomson, while the Norman equivalent of Fitz (from the French-Latin 'filius' meaning 'son') cropped up in Fitzmaurice and Fitzgerald.

The prefix 'Mac' was 'son of' in Gaelic and clans often originated with occupations - as in MacNab being sons of the Abbot, MacPherson and MacVicar being sons of the minister and MacIntosh being sons of the chief.

The church's influence could be found in the names Kirk, Clerk, Clarke, Bishop, Friar and Monk. Proctor came from a church official, Singer and Sangster from choristers, Gilchrist and Gillies from Christ's servant, Mitchell, Gilmory and Gilmour from servants of St Michael and Mary, Malcolm from a servant of Columba and Gillespie from a bishop's servant.

The rudimentary medical profession was represented by Barber (a trade which also once included dentistry and surgery) as well as Leech or Leitch.

Businessmen produced Merchants, Mercers, Monypennies, Chapmans, Sellers and Scales, while down at the old village watermill the names that cropped up included Miller, Walker and Fuller.

Other self explanatory trades included Coopers, Brands, Barkers, Tanners, Skinners, Brewsters and Brewers, Tailors, Saddlers, Wrights, Cartwrights, Smiths, Harpers, Joiners, Sawyers, Masons and Plumbers.

Even the scenery was utilised as in Craig, Moor, Hill, Glen, Wood and Forrest.

Rank, whether high or low, took its place with Laird, Barron, Knight, Tennant, Farmer, Husband, Granger, Grieve, Shepherd, Shearer and Fletcher.

The hunt and the chase supplied Hunter, Falconer, Fowler, Fox, Forrester, Archer and Spearman.

The renowned medieval historian Froissart, who eulogised about the romantic deeds of chivalry (and who condemned Scotland as being a poverty stricken wasteland), once sniffily dismissed the peasantry of his native France as the jacquerie (or the jacques-without-names) but it was these same humble folk who ended up overthrowing the arrogant aristocracy.

In the olden days, only the blueblooded knights of antiquity were entitled to full, proper names, both Christian and surnames, but with the passing of time and a more egalitarian, less feudal atmosphere, more respectful and worthy titles spread throughout the populace as a whole.

Echoes of a far distant past can still be found in most names and they can be borne with pride in commemoration of past generations who fought and toiled in some capacity or other to make our nation what it now is, for good or ill.

Chapter two:

The men from the West

The surnames of Irvine and Irving are virtually interchangeable, with bearers of both versions of the name having played a significant role in the high drama and romance of Scotland's history.

Other forms of the name, including Ervine, Erwing, Irwing, Irwyn, Urwin, and Herwineare are almost as numerous as the various explanations of its origins.

One tradition is that it derives from the ancient Brythonic 'ir afon', meaning 'green water', while an even more colourful theory is that it stems from 'Erinviennes'.

This was the name given to Irish descendants of the High Kings of Ireland who settled on the west coast of Scotland from about the end of the fifth century onwards – with 'Erin' meaning 'from the West', and 'viene' denoting 'a brave and worthy man.'

This tradition further asserts that it was the Erinviennes who gave their name to what is now the thriving royal burgh of Irvine, on the Ayrshire coast.

The tradition may not be as far-fetched as it may first appear, because it links intriguingly to another persistent tradition that the first mention of the name of Irvine in all its various forms in Scottish records concerns a Crinus Ervines.

He was the hereditary abbot of Dunkeld, who traced a descent back through the mists of time to the High Kings of Ireland.

The abbot was also married to a daughter of Malcolm II, who reigned in Scotland between 1005 and 1034.

A form of the name is recorded in Galloway, in the far south of Scotland, in the twelfth century, while a Robert de Herwine is recorded in Dumfriesshire in 1226.

Irving (with a 'g') was also the name of a parish in Dumfriesshire, and it appears that it was at some stage in the fourteenth century that this form became popular in the south of Scotland, while Irvine (with an 'e') became more popular further north.

It was in the north of Scotland, in Aberdeenshire, that a family of Irvines flourished for centuries as the lairds of the Drum, and this family traced a descent from the Irvings of Bonshaw, in Dumfriesshire.

In 1587, an Act of the Scottish Parliament recognised these Irvings of Bonshaw as the 'chiefly family' of the name.

Significant numbers of Irvines settled in Ireland during what was known as the Plantation of Ireland from 1609 to 1613, and one family was responsible for the building of Irvine Castle, in Fermanagh.

In later centuries, many of these Irvines left Ireland to find a new life in North America, while Irvings are known to have left their native Dumfriesshire to settle in Canada.

It is also interesting to note that in both Ireland and North America 'Irvine' tends to be pronounced 'Ir-vine', while the common pronunciation in Scotland is 'Ir-vin'.

Linguistic and spelling differentiations apart, generations of Irvines and Irvings in Scotland played a significant role in both the bitter Wars of Independence with England and the equally bitter trials and tribulations of the Royal House of Stuart.

Foremost among the warriors for Scotland's freedom and independence was William de Irwyn, of the Bonshaw branch of the family in Dumfriesshire.

By 1296, Scotland groaned under the iron grip of English occupation, but William Wallace raised the banner of revolt in May of 1297 after he killed Sir William Heselrig, Sheriff of Lanark, in revenge for the killing of his young wife, Marion.

Proving an expert in the tactics of guerrilla warfare, Wallace and his hardened band of freedom fighters inflicted stunning defeats on the English garrisons.

This culminated in the liberation of practically all of Scotland following the battle of Stirling Bridge, on September 11, 1297.

Defeated at the battle of Falkirk on July 22, 1298, after earlier being appointed Guardian of Scotland, Sir William Wallace was eventually betrayed and captured in August of 1305.

On the black day for Scotland of August 23 of that year, he was brutally executed in London on the orders of a vengeful Edward I of England, better known as 'The Hammer of the Scots'.

Less than a year later, however, Scotland again rose in rebellion – this time under the inspired leadership of Robert the Bruce, who had been enthroned as King of Scots at Scone in March of 1306.

Defeat followed at the battle of Methven in June, however, and Bruce was forced to seek refuge on the inhospitable island of Rathlin, between the west coast of Scotland and the east coast of Ireland.

Returning to Scotland in February of the following year, however, the great warrior king and his stalwart supporters such as William de Irwyn set the nation aflame as, in a succession of daring guerrilla attacks, they inflicted a series of defeats on the English garrisons.

One tradition is that it was after one of his raids on a garrison in the southwest of Scotland that Bruce was forced to flee for his life, closely pursued by the enemy.

Among his small entourage of battle-hardened warriors was Sir William de Irwyn, who is said to have stood guard as the exhausted king took some much-needed rest under a holly tree.

This incident, the tradition holds, gave rise to the Irvine/Irving family crest of a sheaf of holly and the motto 'Flourishing in both sunshine and in shade'.

Sir William fought with distinction at the side of Bruce at the battle Bannockburn in June of 1314, when a 20,000-strong English army under Edward II was defeated by a Scots army less than half this strength.

By midsummer of 1313 the mighty fortress of Stirling Castle was occupied by an English garrison under the command of Sir Philip Mowbray.

Bruce's brother, Edward, had agreed to a pledge by Mowbray that if the castle was not relieved by battle by midsummer of the following year, then he would surrender.

This made battle inevitable, and by June 23 of 1314 the two armies faced one another at Bannockburn, in sight of the castle.

It was on this day that Bruce slew the English knight Sir Henry de Bohun in single combat, but the battle proper was not fought until the following day, shortly after the rise of the midsummer sun.

The English cavalry launched a desperate but futile charge on the densely packed ranks of Scottish spearmen known as schiltrons, and by the time the sun had sank slowly in the west the English army had been totally routed, with Edward himself only narrowly managing to make his escape from the carnage of the battlefield.

Scotland's independence had been secured, to the glory of Bruce and his loyal army and at terrible cost to the English.

In reward for his gallant service to Bruce,

Sir William was granted 10,000 acres of land in Aberdeenshire that were confiscated from Bruce's enemies, the Comyns.

This barony included the Royal Forest of Oaks and the imposing edifice of Drum Castle, the proud possession and stronghold of the Irvine lairds of Drum.

Chapter three:

High honours

Succeeding generations of Irvines and Irvings continued to play a dominant role in Scottish affairs, including the 4th Laird of Drum, who was involved in the lengthy and tortuous negotiations with England to secure the release from captivity of James I.

James had become a pawn in a struggle between powerful nobles and his father Robert III, culminating in him being carried for his own safety to the refuge of the Bass Rock, in the Firth of Forth.

He stayed here for about a month before a merchant vessel picked him up in March of 1406 to take him to a more secure refuge in France, but English pirates captured the ship off Flamborough Head, and the eleven-year-old prince was taken into the custody of England's ambitious and designing Henry V.

Robert III died only a few weeks later,

and the young prince now became James I of Scotland.

It would be 18 long years before he was released from custody, and the 4th Laird of Drum was instrumental in the Treaty of London, signed in December of 1423.

This made arrangements that the king would be released only for a ransom of £40,000, payable over six years, while twenty-one sons of the Scottish nobility were to be taken as hostages until the full amount was paid.

Adding insult to injury, the treaty also stipulated that the hostages should be kept at the expense of their own families, while a further £4,000 was demanded as the cost of the king's upkeep while he had been held captive in England!

James eventually returned to his kingdom in February of 1424, and promptly rewarded the 4th Laird of Drum with a knighthood for his efforts on his monarch's behalf.

On the battlefield, the 3rd Laird of Drum, Sir Alexander Irvine, had thirteen years earlier been involved in one of the most savage battles on Scottish soil.

This was the Battle of Harlaw, fought on July 24, 1411, just north of Aberdeen and in the heart of the Irvines of Drum homeland.

Also known as the Battle of Red Harlaw, it was sparked off when Donald Macdonald, 2nd Lord of the Isles, mustered about 6000 of his best clansmen and burned Inverness after crossing to the mainland and marching up the Great Glen.

His strength swelled to 10,000 after other clansmen including Camerons, Chattans, MacIntoshes, and MacLeods joined him: promising them rich pickings, Macdonald then marched them towards Aberdeen.

The Earl of Mar and his cousin, Sir William Irvine, hastily assembled a force that included other northeast lairds, while the Provost of Aberdeen also raised men.

The opposing forces met just north of Aberdeen, and battle was joined shortly after the summer sun had risen.

The fearless and ferocious clansmen

repeatedly charged the ranks of the Earl of Mar and his men, only to be cut down in swathes, but not before exacting their own toll in blood.

As the sun sank low in the west, both sides were exhausted and had to retire from the fray, leaving behind a battlefield littered with the corpses of at least 1000 clansmen and 600 of Mar's men.

Among the dead was Sir William Irvine, who had engaged in ferocious hand-to-hand combat with the chief of the Macleans of Duart, famously known as Red Hector of the Battles.

At the end of what was described as 'noble and notable single combat', both men lay dead, and Sir William's bravery is commemorated in a ballad, where he is referred to as 'good Sir Alexander Irvine, the much renowned Laird of Drum.'

Further south, the Irvings of Bonshaw, in Dumfriesshire, also distinguished themselves in battle.

Christopher Irving of Bonshaw and one of his sons were among the 5,000 Scots, including James IV, an archbishop, two bishops, eleven earls, fifteen barons, and 300 knights, who were killed at the disastrous battle of Flodden, fought on September 9, 1513.

The Scottish monarch had embarked on the venture after Queen Anne of France, under the terms of the Auld Alliance between Scotland and her nation, appealed to him to 'break a lance' on her behalf and act as her chosen knight.

Crossing the border into England at the head of a 25,000-strong army that included 7,500 clansmen and their kinsmen, James engaged a 20,000-strong force commanded by the Earl of Surrey.

Despite their numerical superiority and bravery, however, the Scots proved no match for the skilled English artillery and superior military tactics of Surrey.

During the destructive civil war between Crown and Covenant, the Irvines proved staunch Royalists, with Drum Castle suffering several times from the depredations of the Covenanters – who supported the National

Covenant of 1638, which pledged to uphold the Presbyterian religion.

Alexander Irvine, the 10th Laird of Drum, was imprisoned on a number of occasions by the Presbyterian authorities for his Royalist stance, while his son, Robert, died a prisoner in Edinburgh's grim Tolbooth in 1646.

The 14th Laird of Drum also proved loyal to the cause of the Royal House of Stuart.

He fought at Sheriffmuir during the abortive Jacobite Rising of 1715, while Alexander Irvine, 17th Laird of Drum, volunteered to serve in the Pitsligo's Horse regiment after Prince Charles Edward Stuart raised the Jacobite standard at Glenfinnan to rally support for the 1745 Rising.

Following the carnage of the battle of Culloden fought on April 16, 1746, and the end of all Jacobite hopes for the restoration of the Stuarts to the throne, the laird was among those for whom arrest warrants had been issued.

Fleeing to Drum Castle, and with the help of his sister, Mary Irvine, he managed to hide for a time in a secret room before escaping to exile in France.

Tried in his absence, he was later acquitted on a technicality, and returned to his Aberdeenshire homeland in about 1753.

Continuing a martial tradition, Colonel John Irving fought for the British Army during the Abyssinian Campaign of 1867, while the 22nd Laird of Drum fought with the elite Grenadier Guards during the First World War.

Colonel John Irving's son, meanwhile, Robert Irving, was the captain of the Queen Mary and commodore of the famous Cunard Line.

Across the Atlantic, William Irvine, born in 1741, was the American of Irish descent who achieved renown as a doctor, soldier, and statesman.

Hailing from Carlisle, in Pennsylvania, he was a Brigadier General in the Continental Army, and represented Pennsylvania in the U.S. House of Representatives from 1793 to 1795.

Chapter four:

Reaching for the summit

Generations of Irvines and Irvings have achieved fame both in Scotland and in the wider international arena.

William Irvine, born in Kilsyth, in Scotland's north Lanarkshire in 1863, was a fiery Presbyterian evangelist who worked in the dirty and dangerous environment of the coalmines before studying at the John Anderson's Bible Training Institute in Glasgow.

From the depths of the coalmines to the snow-capped peaks of the Himalayas, Andrew Irvine was one of the mountaineers who attempted to make the first ascent of Mount Everest in 1924.

Better known as Sandy Irvine, and born in Birkenhead, in England, in 1902, he was a keen sportsman and was selected to make the assault on Everest as a member of a team that included his friend George Mallory.

Irvine and Mallory were last spotted on

June 8, 1924, apparently on course for the summit, but were never heard from again.

Mallory's body was found in 1999, but Irvine's body has never been recovered, and speculation continues as to whether or not the two actually did reach the summit and were killed during their precarious descent.

In the world of literature, Washington Irving, whose father was born in Orkney, was the prolific American essayist whose works include *Tales of a Traveller* and a number of biographies.

On the stage Sir Henry Irving, born in 1838, was the English actor renowned for his memorable roles in a number of Shakespearian plays.

He was also the first British actor to receive the accolade of knighthood.

In the world of contemporary music, Andy Irvine, born in London in 1942 and of Irish-Scottish parentage, is a respected folk musician, singer, and songwriter.

On the motor racing circuit, Eddie Irvine is the former Formula One racing driver who was born in Newtonards, in Ireland, in 1965, and who began his racing career in 1983.

On the rugby pitch, Andy Irvine, born in Edinburgh in 1951, won 51 caps for Scotland, playing as a fullback between 1972 and 1978, and he also holds three British Lions caps.

Also in the world of sport, Hazel Irvine, born in 1965, is a popular Scottish-born sports broadcaster who in 1997 became the youngest ever presenter of the BBC's *Grandstand* programme.

In the world of politics and the law, Alexander Irvine, born in Inverness in 1940, holds the title of Baron Irvine of Lairg.

At one stage in his career as a barrister in England he had the future Prime Minister Tony Blair and Cherie Booth, subsequently Blair's wife, as two of his pupils.

He was appointed to the highly powerful and prestigious post of Lord Chancellor after Blair's election victory in 1997.

Shortly afterwards, he became embroiled in controversy after it was revealed that his official residence in the palace of Westminster had been re-decorated to the tune of more than £0.5million – with hand-painted wallpaper alone costing £59,000.

He retired from his post in June of 2003.

'Irvine', of course, is also the name of the royal burgh situated on the Ayrshire coastline, and for centuries its harbour was regarded as one of the most important in Scotland, while during the Wars of Independence with England the town and its vicinity held vital strategic importance for both sides.

Irvine no longer is classified as a commercial port, but it was classed as a Scottish 'New Town' in 1965 and received much needed development, and is now home to part of the Scottish Maritime Museum.

Scotland's national bard, Robert Burns, had many associations with Irvine, and this explains why two of its streets are named after him.

It was also the home of the late eighteenth and early nineteenth century writer John Galt, author of *Annals of the Parish*.